MASTERING PL-SQL: A COMPREHENSIVE GUIDE FOR DEVELOPERS AND DATABASE ADMINISTRATORS

DR ASHOK JAHAGIRDAR PHD
9INFORMATION TECHNOLOGY)

I dedicate this work to **Pia Saxena**, an extraordinary young mind who has redefined the boundaries of learning in the digital age. At just 13 years of age, Pia embarked on a journey with me, first from the bustling streets of Delhi and later from the vibrant city of New York, where she now resides. Our online classes, though challenging without the aid of a traditional blackboard, became a testament to her remarkable aptitude and determination.

Despite the inherent difficulties of teaching programming in a virtual setting, Pia's rapid mastery of Python was nothing short of astonishing. She not only grasped the intricacies of the language but also demonstrated an exceptional ability to combine algorithms and bring them to life through code. Her intellect and creativity shine through in every line she writes, hinting at a future filled with endless possibilities.

Mind you, she is only 13 years old. Who knows where her journey will take her? But one thing is certain: the world will be watching with bated breath.

Dr Ashok Jahagirdar

August 2024

Contents

CHAPTER ONE

Introduction to PL/SQL

<u>What is PL/SQL?</u>

PL/SQL (Procedural Language/SQL) is a powerful extension of SQL (Structured Query Language) used in Oracle databases. It combines the ease of SQL with the procedural capabilities of programming languages, allowing developers to write code that can interact with the database in a structured, controlled, and efficient manner.

PL/SQL was introduced by Oracle Corporation as part of Oracle Database version 7. The goal was to bridge the gap between SQL and procedural programming by providing a way to execute complex operations on data within the database, using SQL statements combined with procedural constructs like loops, conditionals, and exception handling.

- <u>History and Evolution of PL/SQL</u>

PL/SQL has been a critical component of Oracle Database since its introduction in the late 1980s. Over the years, it has evolved significantly, with new features and enhancements being added in each major release of Oracle Database.

- Oracle 7: Introduction of PL/SQL with basic features like procedures, functions, and triggers.
- Oracle 8i: Addition of object-oriented features, bulk processing, and dynamic SQL.
- Oracle 9i: Introduction of advanced features like LOBs (Large Objects), fine-grained access control, and enhancements to performance and scalability.
- Oracle 10g: Focus on performance tuning, integration with web services, and XML processing capabilities.
- Oracle 11g: Enhancements to error handling, improved performance features, and the introduction of PL/SQL-specific optimizations.
- Oracle 12c and Beyond: Continued enhancements to cloud integration, JSON processing, and tighter integration with other Oracle technologies.

- <u>Why Use PL/SQL?</u>

PL/SQL provides several advantages over traditional SQL, making it an essential tool for developers and database administrators:

- <u>Efficiency:</u>

PL/SQL allows you to process multiple SQL statements in a single block of code, reducing the need for multiple round-trips between the application and the database.

- <u>Modularity:</u>

Code can be organized into reusable units like procedures, functions, and packages, promoting code reuse and maintainability.

- <u>Error Handling:</u>

PL/SQL provides robust error-handling mechanisms, allowing developers to handle exceptions gracefully and ensure the stability of their applications.

- <u>Performance:</u>

PL/SQL's ability to process data in bulk, handle complex logic, and integrate with advanced Oracle features makes it a high-performance solution for database operations.

- <u>Security:</u>

With PL/SQL, you can enforce security measures at the database level, controlling access to data and ensuring compliance with regulatory requirements.

- <u>PL/SQL vs. SQL:</u>

<u>Key Differences</u>
While SQL is a powerful language for querying and manipulating data in a database, it is limited when it comes to procedural logic and complex ope nrations. PL/SQL fills this gap by providing a procedural programming environment within the database.

Features SQL PL/SQL
Type: Declarative Procedural
Execution: Single Statement Block of Statements
Flow Control: Limited (CASE, IF) Full Control Structures
Error Handling: Basic Advanced
Modularity: Limited High (Procedures, Packages)

Performance Query Code
Optimization: Optimization Optimization
Security: Role and Privilege Granular
Management Control

CHAPTER TWO

Setting Up Your Environment

Let us step through the setting up your development environment for PL/SQL. Whether you're a beginner or an experienced developer, these steps will ensure you have all the tools you need to start coding in PL/SQL.

- Installing Oracle Database

To begin with PL/SQL, you'll need access to an Oracle Database. Oracle provides several options for installing the database, including:

- Oracle Database Standard Edition: Ideal for small to medium-sized businesses with basic database needs.
- Oracle Database Enterprise Edition: Suitable for large enterprises with advanced database requirements.
- Oracle Database Express Edition (XE): A free, lightweight version of Oracle Database for learning and small projects.
- Configuring Oracle SQL Developer

Oracle SQL Developer is a free integrated development environment (IDE) for working with Oracle databases. It provides a user-friendly interface for writing and executing

SQL and PL/SQL code, managing database objects, and performing various database administration tasks.

- Steps to configure SQL Developer:

- Download and Install: Obtain SQL Developer from the official Oracle website and install it on your system.
- Create a Database Connection: Set up a connection to your Oracle Database by providing the necessary credentials (hostname, port, service name, username, and password).
- Familiarize Yourself with the Interface: Explore the different views and tools available in SQL Developer, such as the SQL Worksheet, Connections pane, and PL/SQL Editor.
- Connecting to the Database

Before you can start writing PL/SQL code, you need to connect to your Oracle Database instance. This connection allows you to interact with the database, execute SQL and PL/SQL code, and manage database objects.

Example of a basic database connection:

-- Connect to the Oracle Database using SQL*Plus

```
sqlplus          username/password@hostname:port/service_name
```

-- Alternatively, use SQL Developer to connect

- First Steps with PL/SQL

Once connected, you're ready to start writing your first PL/SQL program. Here's a simple example to get you started:

Hello World Program in PL/SQL

```
BEGIN
DBMS_OUTPUT.PUT_LINE('Hello, World!');
END;
```

In this program, we use the DBMS_OUTPUT.PUT_LINE procedure to print "Hello, World!" to the console. This is a basic example, but it illustrates the structure of a PL/SQL block and how to execute simple PL/SQL commands.

CHAPTER THREE

Basic PL/SQL Concepts

In this chapter, let us explore the foundational concepts of PL/SQL, which will help you build a strong base for developing more advanced programs.

Understanding the basics of PL/SQL block structure, variables, data types, control structures, and cursors is essential for effective PL/SQL programming.

- <u>PL/SQL Block Structure</u>

PL/SQL code is organized into blocks, which are the basic units of a PL/SQL program. A PL/SQL block is composed of three sections:

- <u>Declaration Section (Optional)</u>

Used to declare variables, constants, cursors, and exceptions.
Begins with the DECLARE keyword.

- <u>Executable Section (Compulsory)</u>

Contains the actual code to be executed, such as SQL statements, control structures, and procedural logic.

Begins with the BEGIN keyword.

- <u>Exception Handling Section (Optional)</u>

Handles errors or exceptions that occur during the execution of the block.

Begins with the EXCEPTION keyword.

Basic Structure of a PL/SQL Block:

```
DECLARE
-- Declaration of variables, constants, cursors, etc.
v_example NUMBER;
BEGIN
-- Executable statements
v_example := 100;
DBMS_OUTPUT.PUT_LINE('The value of v_example is
' || v_example);
EXCEPTION
-- Exception handling statements
WHEN OTHERS THEN
DBMS_OUTPUT.PUT_LINE('An error occurred.');
END;
```

In this example, the DECLARE section is where variables are defined. The BEGIN section is where the main logic of the program is executed. If an error occurs, the EXCEPTION section will handle it.

- <u>Variables and Data Types</u>

PL/SQL supports a wide range of data types, allowing you to declare variables that can store different types of values. Understanding how to declare and use variables is key to writing effective PL/SQL code.

- <u>Declaring Variables</u>

Variables in PL/SQL are declared in the DECLARE section of a PL/SQL block. The syntax for declaring a variable is as follows:

variable_name data_type [NOT NULL] [:= initial_value];

variable_name: The name of the variable.

data_type: The type of data the variable can hold (e.g., NUMBER, VARCHAR2, DATE).

<u>NOT NULL:</u>

An optional constraint that ensures the variable cannot hold a NULL value.

initial_value: An optional initial value assigned to the variable.

Example:

```
DECLARE
v_employee_id NUMBER(6);
v_employee_name VARCHAR2(50) := 'John Doe';
v_hire_date DATE := SYSDATE;
BEGIN
DBMS_OUTPUT.PUT_LINE('Employee Name:  ' ||
v_employee_name);
DBMS_OUTPUT.PUT_LINE('Hire Date:  ' ||
v_hire_date);
END;
```

In this example, three variables are declared: v_employee_id (a number), v_employee_name (a string), and v_hire_date (a date).

- <u>Common Data Types in PL/SQL</u>

PL/SQL supports various data types, which can be broadly categorized as follows:

- Scalar Data Types: Store a single value (e.g., - NUMBER, VARCHAR2, DATE, BOOLEAN).
- Composite Data Types: Store multiple values (e.g., RECORD, TABLE, VARRAY).
- Reference Data Types: Store pointers to other data items (e.g., REF CURSOR).
- LOB Data Types: Store large objects (e.g., CLOB, BLOB).

- <u>Commonly Used Data Types:</u>

Data Type Description Example Usage

NUMBER Stores numeric values v_salary NUMBER(10,2);

VARCHAR2 Stores variable-length strings v_name VARCHAR2(100);

DATE Stores date and time values v_hire_date DATE;

BOOLEAN Stores TRUE, FALSE or NULL values v_is_active BOOLEAN;

CLOB Stores large text data v_resume CLOB;

BLOB Stores binary data v_image BLOB;

- <u>Control Structures</u>

Control structures allow you to control the flow of execution in a PL/SQL program. They enable you to implement conditional logic, loops, and branching within your code.

- <u>Conditional Statements</u>

PL/SQL provides several ways to implement conditional logic:

IF-THEN Statement:

Executes a block of code if a condition is true.

IF condition THEN

-- Statements to execute if condition is true

END IF;

IF-THEN-ELSE Statement:

Executes one block of code if a condition is true and another block if it is false.

IF condition THEN

-- Statements to execute if condition is true

ELSE

-- Statements to execute if condition is false

END IF;

IF-THEN-ELSIF-ELSE Statement:

Handles multiple conditions.

IF condition1 THEN

-- Statements to execute if condition1 is true

ELSIF condition2 THEN

-- Statements to execute if condition2 is true

ELSE

-- Statements to execute if none of the conditions are true

END IF;

CASE Statement:

Provides a more concise way to handle multiple conditions.

CASE expression

WHEN value1 THEN

-- Statements to execute if expression = value1

WHEN value2 THEN

-- Statements to execute if expression = value2

```
ELSE
-- Statements to execute if no match is found
END CASE;
Example:
DECLARE
v_grade CHAR(1) := 'A';
BEGIN
CASE v_grade
WHEN 'A' THEN
DBMS_OUTPUT.PUT_LINE('Excellent!');
WHEN 'B' THEN
DBMS_OUTPUT.PUT_LINE('Good');
ELSE
DBMS_OUTPUT.PUT_LINE('Needs Improvement');
END CASE;
END;
```

- ## Looping Structures

Loops allow you to execute a block of code multiple times. PL/SQL supports several types of loops:

- ## Basic LOOP:

Executes a block of code indefinitely until an EXIT statement is encountered.

```
LOOP
-- Statements to execute
EXIT WHEN condition;
END LOOP;
```

WHILE LOOP:

Repeats a block of code as long as a condition is true.

```
WHILE condition LOOP
```

```
-- Statements to execute
END LOOP;
```

FOR LOOP:

Repeats a block of code a specified number of times.

```
FOR i IN 1..10 LOOP
-- Statements to execute
END LOOP;
```

Example:

```
DECLARE
v_counter NUMBER := 1;
BEGIN
WHILE v_counter <= 5 LOOP
DBMS_OUTPUT.PUT_LINE('Counter: ' || v_counter);
v_counter := v_counter + 1;
END LOOP;
END;
```

In this example, the loop prints the value of v_counter five times, incrementing the counter with each iteration.

- ### Working with Cursors

Cursors allow you to fetch and process query results row by row. They are especially useful when dealing with large datasets or when you need to perform operations on each row individually.

- Implicit Cursors

Oracle automatically creates an implicit cursor for every SQL SELECT statement that returns a single row. These cursors are managed by Oracle, and you don't need to explicitly define or control them.

Example:

```
DECLARE
v_employee_name VARCHAR2(50);
```

```
BEGIN
SELECT first_name INTO v_employee_name
FROM employees
WHERE employee_id = 101;
DBMS_OUTPUT.PUT_LINE('Employee   Name:   '   ||
v_employee_name);
END;
```

In this example, an implicit cursor is used to fetch the first name of an employee with a specific ID.

- Explicit Cursors

Explicit cursors give you more control over the processing of query results. You need to declare, open, fetch, and close the cursor manually.

Steps to Use an Explicit Cursor:

1. Declare the Cursor:

Define the query that the cursor will execute.

```
CURSOR cursor_name IS
SELECT column1, column2
FROM table_name
WHERE condition;
```

2. Open the Cursor:

Initialize the cursor and execute the query.

```
OPEN cursor_name;
```

3. Fetch Data:

Retrieve each row from the result set into variables.

```
FETCH cursor_name INTO variable1, variable2;
```

4.Close the Cursor:

Release the memory and resources associated with the cursor.

```
CLOSE cursor_name;
```

Example:

```
DECLARE
CURSOR c_employees IS
```

```
SELECT first_name, last_name
FROM employees;
v_first_name employees.first_name%TYPE;
v_last_name employees.last_name%TYPE;
BEGIN
OPEN c_employees;
LOOP
FETCH       c_employees       INTO       v_first_name,
v_last_name;
EXIT WHEN c_employees%NOTFOUND;
DBMS_OUTPUT.PUT_LINE('Employee:         '         ||
v_first_name || ' ' || v_last_name);
END LOOP;
CLOSE c_employees;
END;
```

In this example, an explicit cursor c_employees is declared to fetch the first and last names of all employees. The cursor is opened, each row is fetched in a loop, and the cursor is closed after processing all the rows.

This chapter provides the foundation you need to start writing PL/SQL programs. By mastering these basic concepts, you'll be well-prepared to tackle more advanced topics in PL/SQL.

CHAPTER FOUR

Advanced PL/SQL Constructs

During our PL/SQL journey, understanding advanced constructs will allow us to create more complex, efficient, and modular code. This chapter dives into procedures, functions, packages, triggers, exception handling, and bulk processing, which are key components that elevate your PL/SQL programming to the next level.

- **<u>Procedures and Functions</u>**

Procedures and functions are reusable program units that encapsulate a specific task or set of operations. They promote code reuse, improve maintainability, and make your PL/SQL programs more modular.

<u>- Procedures</u>

A procedure is a subprogram that performs a specific action. It can accept parameters and execute SQL or PL/SQL statements, but it does not return a value directly.

Syntax for Creating a Procedure:

```
CREATE [OR REPLACE] PROCEDURE procedure_name
```

```
[  (parameter_1 [IN | OUT | IN OUT] datatype,
parameter_2 [IN | OUT | IN OUT] datatype, ...) ]
   IS
   -- Declaration section (optional)
   BEGIN
   -- Executable section
   -- SQL and PL/SQL statements
   EXCEPTION
   -- Exception handling section (optional)
   END procedure_name;
```

IN: The parameter is passed into the procedure.

OUT: The procedure can modify the parameter and pass the result back to the caller.

IN OUT: The parameter is passed into the procedure, modified, and passed back out.

Example of a Simple Procedure:

```
CREATE OR REPLACE PROCEDURE raise_salary (
p_employee_id IN employees.employee_id%TYPE,
p_increase_amount IN NUMBER
) IS
BEGIN
UPDATE employees
SET salary = salary + p_increase_amount
WHERE employee_id = p_employee_id;
END raise_salary;
```

This procedure raise_salary accepts an employee ID and an increase amount, then updates the employee's salary accordingly.

Executing the Procedure:

```
BEGIN
raise_salary(101, 500);
END;
```

<u>- Functions</u>

A function is similar to a procedure but differs in one key aspect: it returns a value. Functions can be used in SQL statements, unlike procedures.

Syntax for Creating a Function:

CREATE [OR REPLACE] FUNCTION function_name

[(parameter_1 [IN | OUT | IN OUT] datatype, parameter_2 [IN | OUT | IN OUT] datatype, ...)]

RETURN return_datatype

IS

-- Declaration section (optional)

BEGIN

-- Executable section

-- SQL and PL/SQL statements

RETURN return_value;

EXCEPTION

-- Exception handling section (optional)

END function_name;

Example of a Simple Function:

CREATE OR REPLACE FUNCTION get_employee_salary (

p_employee_id IN employees.employee_id%TYPE

) RETURN NUMBER IS

v_salary employees.salary%TYPE;

BEGIN

SELECT salary INTO v_salary

FROM employees

WHERE employee_id = p_employee_id;

RETURN v_salary;

END get_employee_salary;

This function get_employee_salary accepts an employee ID and returns the salary of the corresponding employee.

Using the Function:

```
DECLARE
v_salary NUMBER;
BEGIN
v_salary := get_employee_salary(101);
DBMS_OUTPUT.PUT_LINE('Salary: ' || v_salary);
END;
```

You can also use functions in SQL queries:

```
SELECT get_employee_salary(101) FROM dual;
```

- ## Packages: Creating and Using

Packages are a way to group related procedures, functions, variables, and other PL/SQL constructs into a single unit. They help organize your code, enhance reusability, and improve performance by loading all package components into memory at once.

- Creating a Package Specification

The package specification (spec) declares the public elements of the package, such as procedures, functions, and variables, that are accessible outside the package.

Syntax for Creating a Package Specification:

```
CREATE [OR REPLACE] PACKAGE package_name IS
-- Declarations of procedures, functions, variables, etc.
END package_name;
```

Example:

```
CREATE OR REPLACE PACKAGE employee_management IS
PROCEDURE raise_salary (p_employee_id IN NUMBER, p_increase_amount IN NUMBER);
FUNCTION get_employee_salary (p_employee_id IN NUMBER) RETURN NUMBER;
END employee_management;
```

- Creating a Package Body

The package body defines the implementation of the procedures, functions, and other elements declared in the specification. It is where the actual code resides.

Syntax for Creating a Package Body:

CREATE [OR REPLACE] PACKAGE BODY package_name IS

-- Implementations of procedures, functions, etc.

END package_name;

Example:

CREATE OR REPLACE PACKAGE BODY employee_management IS

PROCEDURE raise_salary (p_employee_id IN NUMBER, p_increase_amount IN NUMBER) IS

BEGIN

UPDATE employees

SET salary = salary + p_increase_amount

WHERE employee_id = p_employee_id;

END raise_salary;

FUNCTION get_employee_salary (p_employee_id IN NUMBER) RETURN NUMBER IS

v_salary employees.salary%TYPE;

BEGIN

SELECT salary INTO v_salary

FROM employees

WHERE employee_id = p_employee_id;

RETURN v_salary;

END get_employee_salary;

END employee_management;

You can now use the package's procedures and functions as follows:

BEGIN

employee_management.raise_salary(101, 500);

```
  DBMS_OUTPUT.PUT_LINE('Salary:              '          ||
employee_management.get_employee_salary(101));
  END;
```

- ## **Triggers: Before, After, Instead of**

Triggers are special types of PL/SQL programs that automatically execute in response to specific events on a table or view. They are useful for enforcing business rules, auditing changes, and maintaining complex data integrity.-

- Types of Triggers

- **BEFORE Triggers:** Execute before the triggering event (INSERT, UPDATE, DELETE) occurs.
- **AFTER Triggers:** Execute after the triggering event occurs.
- **INSTEAD OF** Triggers: Execute instead of the triggering event, typically used with views.

- Creating a Trigger

Syntax for Creating a Trigger:

```
CREATE [OR REPLACE] TRIGGER trigger_name
{BEFORE | AFTER | INSTEAD OF} {INSERT | UPDATE | DELETE}
ON table_name
[FOR EACH ROW]
BEGIN
-- Trigger logic
END trigger_name;
```

Example: BEFORE INSERT Trigger:

```
CREATE      OR      REPLACE      TRIGGER
before_employee_insert
```

```
BEFORE INSERT ON employees
FOR EACH ROW
BEGIN
IF :NEW.salary < 3000 THEN
:NEW.salary := 3000; -- Ensure minimum salary
END IF;
END before_employee_insert;
```

This trigger ensures that any new employee inserted into the employees table has a salary of at least 3000.

- Using INSTEAD OF Triggers

INSTEAD OF triggers are used perform operations on views that cannot be modified directly.

Example: INSTEAD OF Trigger on a View:

```
CREATE OR REPLACE VIEW employee_view AS
SELECT employee_id, first_name, last_name
FROM employees;
CREATE OR REPLACE TRIGGER instead_of_employee_view
INSTEAD OF INSERT ON employee_view
BEGIN
INSERT INTO employees (employee_id, first_name, last_name)
VALUES (:NEW.employee_id, :NEW.first_name, :NEW.last_name);
END instead_of_employee_view;
```

This trigger allows you to insert data into a view that is based on a single table.

- **Exception Handling**

Exception handling in PL/SQL is a mechanism to manage runtime errors. Proper exception handling ensures your program can recover from unexpected situations gracefully.

- <u>**Types of Exceptions**</u>
- <u>Predefined Exceptions:</u>

Oracle provides a set of predefined exceptions that cover common errors, such as NO_DATA_FOUND, TOO_MANY_ROWS, and ZERO_DIVIDE.

- <u>User-Defined Exceptions:</u>

You can define your custom exceptions using the EXCEPTION keyword.

- Handling Exceptions

Syntax for Exception Handling:

```
BEGIN
-- Executable statements
EXCEPTION
WHEN exception_name1 THEN
-- Statements to handle exception_name1
WHEN exception_name2 THEN
-- Statements to handle exception_name2
WHEN OTHERS THEN
-- Statements to handle all other exceptions
END;
```

Example of Exception Handling:

```
DECLARE
v_salary employees.salary%TYPE;
BEGIN
SELECT salary INTO v_salary
FROM employees
WHERE employee_id = 999; -- Non-existent employee ID
EXCEPTION
WHEN NO_DATA_FOUND THEN
DBMS_OUTPUT.PUT_LINE('No employee found with that ID.');
```

WHEN OTHERS THEN
DBMS_OUTPUT.PUT_LINE('An unexpected error occurred.');
END;

<u>- User-Defined Exceptions</u>

You can create your exceptions to handle specific error conditions in your application.

Example of User-Defined Exception:

DECLARE
e_salary_too_high EXCEPTION;
v_salary employees.salary%TYPE := 20000;
BEGIN
IF v_salary > 15000 THEN
RAISE e_salary_too_high;
END IF;